Alphabets and Other Writing Systems

by S. Michele McFadden
Illustrated by Derek Ring

PEARSON

Scott
Foresman

Editorial Offices: Glenview, Illinois • Parsippany, New Jersey • New York, New York
Sales Offices: Needham, Massachusetts • Duluth, Georgia • Glenview, Illinois
Coppell, Texas • Sacramento, California • Mesa, Arizona

Today, most people all over the world know how to write. They can put ideas on paper or in e-mails by writing. In English, Spanish, Hmong, and many other languages, people use letters, numbers, and punctuation to write. But people have not always used this system to write.

Pictographs

The first people who wrote did not use letters, words, and punctuation. Thousands of years ago, they "wrote" by making pictures that now are called *pictographs*. Experts say that these pictographs gave information to other people.

Pictographs made by ancient Mayans

---

punctuation: marks used by writers, such as a period (.), comma (,), and question mark (?)

system: organized way of doing things

How do we know about pictographs? Some were drawn on the walls of caves, and they are still there today. We do not know who "wrote" the ideas by using pictographs. We do not know how their language sounded. We *do* know that people in different parts of the world made pictographs. Long, long ago they wrote with pictures. These pictures have been found in modern times when ancient pots, shells, and other things are found under ground.

Extend Language — Greek and Latin Roots

The word *pictograph* is easy to understand if you know its two roots: *pict* and *graph*. *Pictograph* means "a sign used in picture writing." The root *pict* comes from a Latin word for picture. Look at the chart below to find the meaning of *graph*. *Graph* comes from a Greek word. Use a dictionary to find out the meanings of the words *autograph, paragraph,* and *pictoral*.

Root	Meaning	Example
graph	writing	para*graph*
pict	picture	*pict*oral

Pictographs were symbols. Sometimes they represented whole words and other times they represented syllables, or parts of a word. Thousands of years ago, the ancient Sumerian people invented one form of pictographs. In an ancient Sumerian language, *ti* means "arrow." *Ti* (or *til*) also means "life." So Sumerians used an arrow for both words.

This is the Sumerian symbol *ti* or *til*. It can mean "arrow" or "life."

Egyptian Hieroglyphs

Thousands of years ago, the ancient Egyptians also invented their own form of writing called *hieroglyphics*. They used hieroglyphs as a kind of writing. They sometimes put two or more pictures together to "write" a word.

These Egyptian hieroglyphs mean "trouble."

For many years, no one could read Egyptian hieroglyphs. Then, in 1822, a Frenchman named Jean-François Champollion began to uncover their meanings. He worked for years, and finally he translated them. This is what he learned:

Sometimes a hieroglyph stands for a word.

This hieroglyph is the word *rope*.

Sometimes a hieroglyph stands for a sound.

This is the hieroglyph that stands for the sound of the English letter *p*.

Sometimes hieroglyphs are combined to stand for a word.

This hieroglyph is the word *glory*. It has the hieroglyph for *rope* in it.

This is the hieroglyph that stands for the sound of the English letter *t*.

This is the hieroglyph that stands for the sound of the English letter *w*.

To understand ancient Egyptian writing, you need to read the hieroglyphs in all three ways.

Mayan Hieroglyphs

The ancient Mayans of Mexico used hieroglyphs too. Some Mayan hieroglyphs stand for whole words. Other Mayan hieroglyphs stand for sounds or syllables.

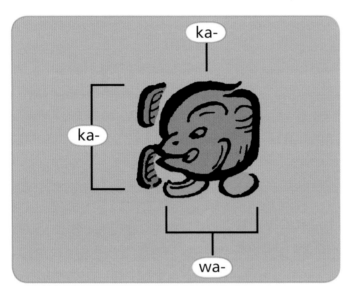

ka-

ka-

wa-

A Mayan hieroglyph: *kakawa*. In Mayan, *ka* and *wa* are syllables.

The main hieroglyph here is a fish head, which stands for the syllable *ka*. The hieroglyphs on the side and bottom stand for syllables too. Together they stand for the Mayan word that is pronounced something like *kakaw*. The English word for *kakaw* is *cacao* or *chocolate*.

Did You Know? What Is a Syllable?

A syllable is a unit of sound in a word. For example, take a look at the English word *sister*. The word *sister* has two syllables. Say *sister*. Can you hear the syllables?

Writing With Alphabets

Today, most writing systems use alphabets. An alphabet is a list of letters used to write in that language. Not all written languages use the same letters. For example, the Spanish alphabet has the letter ñ. The English alphabet does not have this letter. Instead, it uses two letters to make ñ: *n* and *y,* as in *canyon.*

Alphabets for different languages can have different numbers of letters. The English alphabet has twenty-six letters. The Spanish alphabet has twenty-seven letters. The Russian alphabet has thirty-three letters, and the Korean alphabet has twenty-four letters.

This English letter stands for the *t* sound like in the word "tall."

This Spanish letter stands for the *ny* sound in English. The symbol above the *n* is called *tilde* in Spanish.

This Russian letter stands for the *ch* sound like in the English word "chip."

This Korean letter stands for the *ch* sound like in the English word "child."

The Study of Ancient Writing Continues

Today writing systems use alphabets and symbols that are known, but scholars still continue to study the writings of the ancient cultures. Thanks to Jean-François Champollion, people today can read Egyptian hieroglyphs. Scholars are still working to understand Mayan hieroglyphs.

Would you like to be able to translate ancient writings?